BLAST OFF!
EARTH

Helen and David Orme

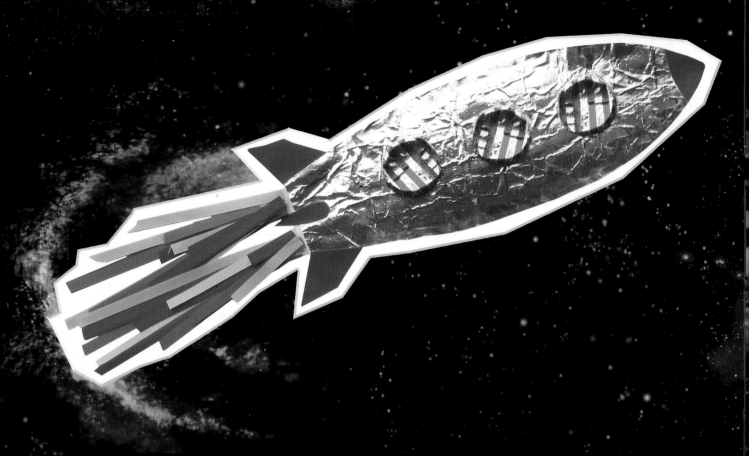

Copyright © ticktock Entertainment Ltd 2007
First published in Great Britain in 2007 by ticktock Media Ltd.,
The Old Sawmill, 103 Goods Station Road,
Tunbridge Wells, Kent, TN1 2DP

ticktock project editor: Julia Adams
ticktock project designer: Emma Randall

We would like to thank: Sandra Voss, Tim Bones, James Powell,
Indexing Specialists (UK) Ltd.

ISBN 978 1 84696 046 8 pbk
ISBN 978 1 84696 548 7 hbk
Printed in China
9 8 7 6 5 4 3
A CIP catalogue record for this book is available from the British Library.

Picture credits
t=top, b=bottom, c=centre, l=left, r=right, bg=background
Corbis: 15bl, 21tl; NASA: 13bl, 21br; Science Photo Library: 4/5bg (original); Shutterstock: front cover, 1tl, 1br, 2/3bg, 8b, 9tl, 9tr,
9cr, 9br, 11b, 12b, 16c, 18b, 19bl, 22cl, 24bg; ticktock picture archive: 5tr, 6bl, 6/7bg, 7tr, 7b, 10bl, 10/11bg, 11tl, 13tr, 14bl,
14/15bg, 15tr, 17tr, 17bl, 17br, 18/19bg, 19tr, 20c, 22cr, 22/23bg, 23tl, 23bl, 23br
Every effort has been made to trace the copyright holders, and we apologise in advance for any unintentional omissions.
We would be pleased to insert the appropriate acknowledgements in any subsequent edition of this publication.

Contents

Where is Earth?

There are eight planets in our solar system. The planets travel around the Sun. Earth is the third planet from the Sun.

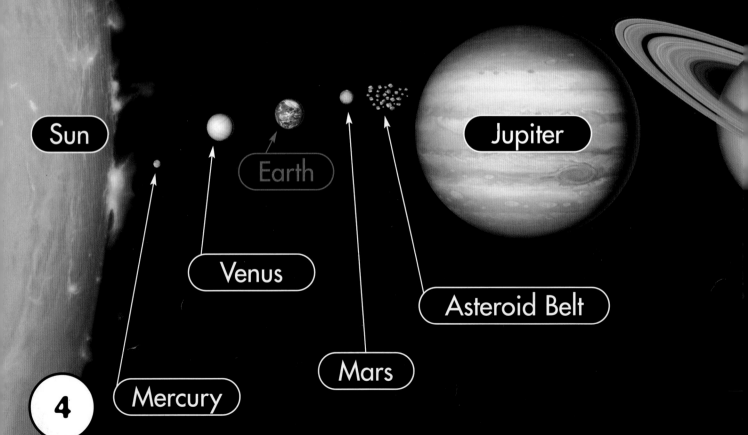

Sun

Earth

Jupiter

Venus

Asteroid Belt

Mars

Mercury

Earth's orbit

Earth travels round the Sun once every 365 days. This journey around the Sun is called Earth's **orbit**. The time a planet takes to orbit the Sun once is called a year.

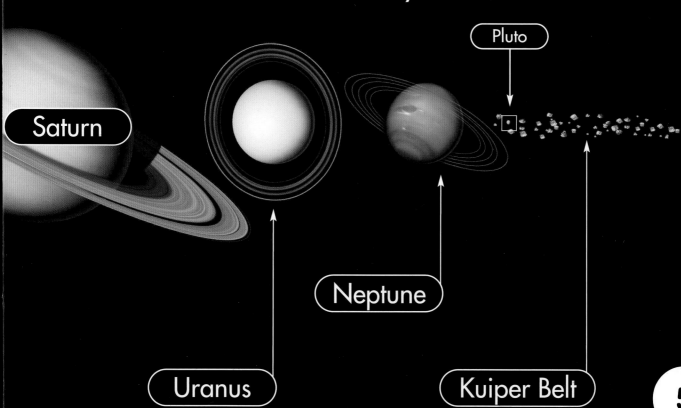

Saturn

Pluto

Neptune

Uranus

Kuiper Belt

Planet Facts

The Earth is the only known planet in our **solar system** with **liquid** water on its surface. Over $^3/_4$ of our planet is covered by water.

Planets are always spinning. A day is the time it takes a planet to spin around once. A day on Earth is 24 hours long.

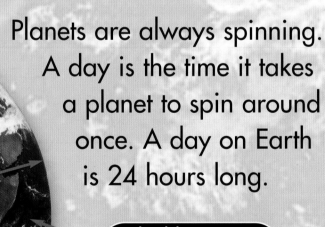

12,756 kilometres

Earth

The blue areas are water

The brown areas are land

The white areas are clouds

This artwork shows the Earth as it spins around. One half of the planet faces away from the Sun. It is in the dark. The other half is in the sunlight.

The Earth has two places called poles: the North Pole and the South Pole. These are at the top and bottom of the planet. The Sun does not shine very strongly at the Poles, so they are cold and icy all year.

Earth is the only planet we know about where people, animals and plants can live. Life is possible on Earth because it has **liquid** water.

The most important thing needed for life is water. But Earth is perfect for life in other ways, too.

Earth has an **atmosphere** with **oxygen**. Almost all living things need oxygen to breathe and survive.

Some places on Earth have very extreme temperatures. But most of Earth is neither too hot nor too cold for life.

60°C
50°C
40°C
30°C
20°C
10°C
0°C
-10°C
-20°C
-30°C
-40°C
-50°C
-60°C
-70°C
-80°C
-90°C

The hottest place on Earth is Al 'Aziziyah, Libya, in Africa. Temperatures can go up to 58°C here.

This is 0°C. It is the temperature when water freezes.

The coldest temperatures are in Antarctica. One time the temperature went down to -89°C here!

The layer of gases that make up the Earth's **atmosphere** is called air. It covers the planet. Because air moves around we have different sorts of weather in different places.

When the air moves we have wind. The wind can be very powerful. Along with water, the wind has made this rock into a strange shape by wearing it away.

Strong winds can cause a lot of damage to buildings and trees.

Wind also moves clouds around the planet. Clouds are made up of millions of very tiny water droplets. These droplets can join together to make bigger drops. If these drops get big and heavy enough, they fall down as rain.

Changing Temperatures

Earth is perfect for life, because it is not too hot or too cold. But **scientists** think that the **temperatures** on Earth are changing.

smoke with carbon dioxide

When we burn oil or coal, we make a gas called **carbon dioxide**. The amount of this gas in our **atmosphere** is growing.

Carbon dioxide trapped in the Earth's atmosphere stops heat escaping from Earth. Scientists think that the trapped gases will slowly make the Earth heat up.

atmosphere

heat waves

surface

Temperature change has already happened on the planet Venus. This planet has heated up so much that it is much too hot and dry for life.

The Earth's Crust

Planet Earth is a huge
ball of rock. It is made of four layers.
The centre of the Earth is called its core.
The inside of the planet is very hot.

Earth has an inner and an outer
core. They are mainly made
of **iron**. The inner core is
the hottest part of Earth.

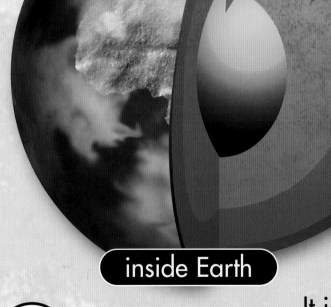

inside Earth

This layer is the
mantle. It is made
of red-hot rock.
Some of it is
molten rock.

The crust of the Earth
is the part that we live on.
It is made up of land and oceans.
It floats on top of the mantle.

The Earth's crust is split into sections called **plates**. The plates are moving very slowly all the time.

The red lines on this map show the edges of the plates. They fit together like a jigsaw puzzle!

Sometimes, when the plates move, the Earth shakes so much that the ground shudders and cracks. We call this an earthquake.

The Earth's surface is covered in mountains and valleys. Earth's highest mountain is Mount Everest. It is 8,850 metres high!

Mount Everest is so high, its top is sometimes higher than the clouds!

Mountains are made by the movement of the Earth's **plates**. When two plates push against each other, they sometimes create a mountain by pushing layers of rock up. This is how Mount Everest was created. It takes millions of years for this to happen.

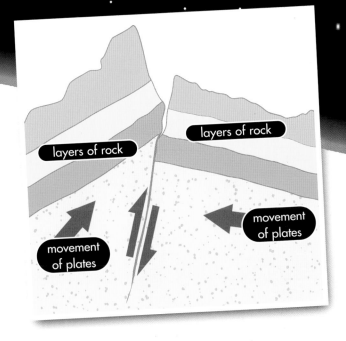

layers of rock

layers of rock

movement of plates

movement of plates

molten rock

volcano

plates

Sometimes when the Earth's plates move, an opening appears in the crust. The hot, **molten rock** from inside the Earth bursts to the surface. This is called a volcano.

The Moon and Satellites

The Moon is a big rock that **orbits** Earth. Objects that orbit a planet are called **satellites**. The Moon is Earth's only natural satellite.

As seen from Earth, the Moon is the brightest object in the **solar system** after the Sun. We can see it without a telescope.

satellite being launched on a rocket

The Earth has many other satellites. These satellites have been launched into space by rockets. They have many different uses.

satellite orbiting Earth

Satellites are used to show television programmes and connect mobile phone calls. Some satellites can give us information about the Earth's weather and warn us of **hurricanes**.

Earth in History

Hundreds of years ago, most people believed that the Earth was flat. They believed that you could fall off the edge of the Earth!

edge of Earth

This map shows Europe and where people believed the edge of the Earth was.

Europe

map from 1492

When **astronomers** saw the other planets were round, they realised that Earth had to be round too.

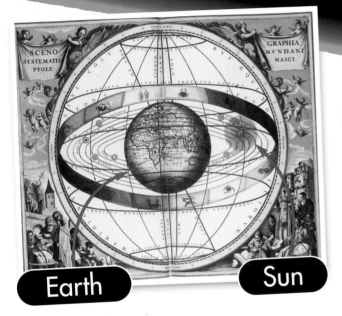

Earth   Sun

People also used to think that the Sun went around the Earth. Today we know it is the other way round.

This picture was painted in 1660, over 300 years ago. It shows the Sun **orbiting** the Earth.

With space travel and the use of satellites, we can see that the Earth orbits around the Sun. This photograph of Earth was taken in 1968 by **astronauts** travelling to the Moon.

Moon's surface

Exploring Earth

We **still don't know**
everything there is to know about
Earth. But **satellites** and **robots**
help us find out more about our planet.

Sahara Desert

Satellites can take photographs of wide areas of land.
This helps us make very exact maps of large regions
of the Earth. It also allows us to see what the Earth
looks like from space.

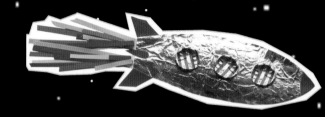

Robots can be used to explore and take pictures of the deepest parts of the ocean.

Some robots look for **oil** and **minerals**.

Some robots can study animals that live in the deepest oceans, such as this fish.

Glossary

Asteroid A rocky object that orbits the Sun. Most asteroids orbit the Sun between Mars and Jupiter.

Astronaut A person trained to travel or work in space.

Astronomer A person who studies space, often using telescopes.

Atmosphere The gases that surround a star, planet or moon.

Carbon dioxide A gas that is made when something burns.

Hurricane The largest, strongest storm on Earth. It forms over an ocean and its high winds join in a circle.

Iron A very hard and strong metal.

Liquid Something that flows easily.

Minerals Material from the Earth that is not a plant or an animal. Gold, silver, iron and salt are all minerals.

Molten rock Rock that has been melted and flows like a liquid.

Oil A greasy liquid that many machines need in order to work.

Orbit The path that a planet or other object takes around the Sun, or the path a satellite takes around a planet.

Oxygen One of the gases in the Earth's atmosphere that we breathe. People and animals need oxygen to live.

Plates The separate pieces that make up the Earth's crust. They float very slowly over liquid rock.

Satellite A moon or a man-made object that is in orbit around a planet.

Solar system The Sun and everything that is in orbit around it.

Temperature How hot or cold something is.

Index